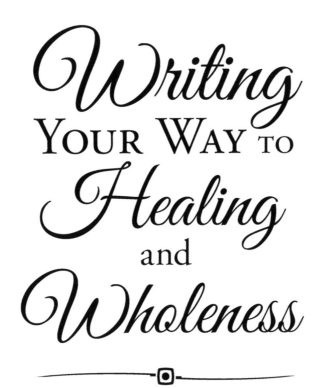

Writing Your Way to Healing and Wholeness

SIMPLE EXERCISES:
EXPLORING YOUR PAST - CHANGING YOUR FUTURE

ROBIN B. DILLEY, PhD

BALBOA.
PRESS
A DIVISION OF HAY HOUSE

Balboa Press books may be ordered through booksellers or by contacting:

Balboa Press
A Division of Hay House
1663 Liberty Drive
Bloomington, IN 47403
www.balboapress.com
1 (877) 407-4847

ISBN: 978-1-5043-6966-4 (sc)
ISBN: 978-1-5043-6967-1 (e)

Library of Congress Control Number: 2016919036

Print information available on the last page.

Balboa Press rev. date: 01/21/2017

Enter

to

the

Pages

of

Your Personal Journey ...

Cover Design: The Labyrinth and the Pen

The labyrinth is an ancient symbol and spiritual tool that allows you to put one foot in front of the other, deliberately and meditatively. This Journal is a metaphorical labyrinth allowing you to walk inside of yourself, exploring the many pathways of your journey. Take a walk into your past by using a pen to let go of old wounds and hurts with your parents, siblings and past situations. Along the "walk," you will gather insight as to how you adopted patterns and behaviors like anger, sadness, helplessness, and defensive stances. The writing exercises inside of these pages, designed to help you to let go of old dysfunctional patterns, will help you transform and grow into new uplifting patterns that promote a healthy sense of self. You will begin acquiring what you desire in life as you walk into your past life while staying present to today.

As you reflect on the reality of your life's journey as a metaphorical labyrinth, one path in and the same path back out again, you might find yourself curious enough to experience a labyrinth walk. You can find a labyrinth near you by going to www. labyrintlocator.com and entering your zip code.

"The Labyrinth is a spiritual tool that has many applications in various settings. It reduces stress, quiets the mind and opens the heart. It is a walking meditation, a path of prayer, and a blue-print where psyche meets Spirit." Artress, Dr. Lauren. *Walking a Sacred Path: Rediscovering the Labyrinth as a Spiritual Practice.* New York: Riverhead Books, 2006

"As you embark on your psychotherapy journey, may you awaken those parts of you that have fallen asleep, open the parts of you that are thirsty, and discover anew the magic of growing."

R.B. Dilley

Foreword

Robin B. Dilley, PhD, is a licensed clinical psychologist, consultant, author, speaker, and workshop facilitator in Phoenix, Arizona.

Dr. Dilley's specialty is in family systems theory. Her practice explicitly emphasizes personal development and redirection. With thirty-five years' experience working with people's unique stories, Dr. Dilley's eclectic approach to psychotherapy centers on the healing relationship between the therapist and the client. By understanding each client's individual and distinctive stories, Dr. Dilley builds a trusting, intuitive relationship, which enables her to use her professional resources with precision to achieve the personal growth desired by her clients.

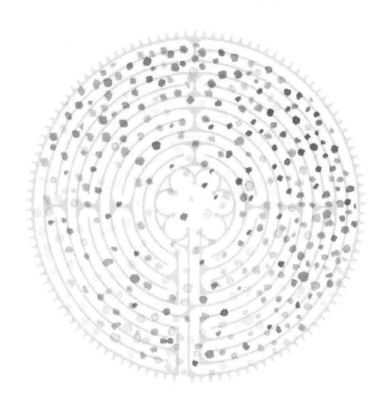

Introduction

Dear Writer,

I believe that we must overcome and resolve the patterns of our past in order to live full and vibrant lives in the present. My passion—assisting my clients to explore and re-examine patterns developed over time—helps them cope and adapt to life's situations. This process eliminates unhelpful patterns that deter them from their personal growth. This journal is the first of several designed to help any person who chooses to take that first step into the labyrinth of personal change.

I have chosen this journal format for several reasons. First, I understand how difficult it is to place hard, cold words onto blank paper. Once you begin a personal journey, issues may come to the surface quickly, creating emotional turmoil and internal chatter. I believe getting that chatter onto paper will help clear your thought patterns and provide the emotional safety and clarity to proceed down the path of personal redirection. I encourage my clients and anyone interested in personal change to write it out. Based on years of experience, I believe writing is one of the best tools to facilitate healing while providing an opportunity for recording goals, dreams, ideas, and new ways of being in the world. Discarding the old habits of *doing* allows room for the new person to emerge and live in the enjoyment of experiencing love, life, and wholeness.

The format of this journal is designed to help you follow a consistent path. The journal begins with writing a letter to yourself. This gives you many opportunities to capture on paper why you are taking this journey now and what you hope to heal and change as a part of the process. You are asked to record three wishes, permitting you to dream about what your best life looks like. The questions that follow are designed to help you pay attention to what gets in the way of making those wishes come true. There are several inserts throughout to assist you in staying on your journey. In addition, each set of questions is designed to take you deeper and wider into exploring yourself, your assets, and your limitations. The journal ends with a letter to yourself that allows you to review your growth and decide where or what to attend to next.

This journal is dedicated to those who are beginning their healing journey on their own. However, it is possible you have been at psychotherapy for a while but never really tackled the source from which your issues derived. In either case, these family-of-origin issues affect you as an adult, and this book will be a welcomed asset on your journey. You can use it with the help of a trained professional or as an adjunctive tool to assist you on your path.

If at any point you choose to work with a professional along the way, the best way to find a good psychotherapist is to simply ask someone who is already seeing one. The second way is to check with your family practice doctor. The third is to call your local American and Family Therapist or Licensed Psychological Associations and ask for a referral in your area. And remember, if you are not comfortable with the person you choose within three sessions, keep looking. Nothing can slow, hurt, or damage your journey of personal growth more quickly than a bad therapeutic match. May you enjoy this process and find it a useful tool for your own personal growth and healing.

The best way to reach me with questions or comments about this journal is at drrobinbdilley@gmail.com. Follow us on Facebook at www.facebook.com/inamomentsnotice.com for daily inspiration and reflection!

Instructions for
Personal Development and Redirection

A Beginner's Journey of Self-Discovery

Within this workbook, you may find helpful exercises for becoming acquainted with yourself, especially in the form of a journal. Journal writing is despised by many who would otherwise enjoy a personal-development exercise. Staring at a piece of white paper can be intimidating and even feel a bit demanding. We do not always know how to start writing down our feelings or how to explore them in ways that bring about positive changes. As a result, we say nothing and feel nothing, dropping once again into an abyss of nothingness. This journal is designed to help you explore yourself, your feelings, and your family issues. It invites you to use it as a tool to facilitate questions and feelings. Below, I have listed some ideas and guidelines to help you develop a safe place to explore who you are and how you are changing. Emotional safety is a necessity for personal growth and change. Until you feel safe, you will likely keep old defenses up, protecting yourself from new and perhaps better ways of living your life.

Create a Space in Your Life for Personal Development and Redirection

A. Choose a special place to write, think, and pray. This can be a designated area in your home, a favorite coffee bar, or a park. It can be anywhere that calls you to self-discovery by providing an atmosphere that allows you to relax and be you. If it is a special space in your home, place some items or symbols that will help you take the leap into creativity. If you prefer to go out to write, then make a special bag that carries your journal, crayons, bubbles, special pens, and perhaps even a favorite book. Keep the bag in your car so that you can write whenever the opportunity arises.

B. Read fairy tales, children's stories, and inspirational material to keep you motivated. Arouse early childhood feelings and memories while fertilizing your unconscious with the rich symbols and metaphors of stories.

C. Set aside time each day that is just for you. Don't allow anyone else a vote about what you do with this time. For those of you who are incredibly busy, this set-aside time may be as little as fifteen minutes. But make the time, and guard it like a protective mother tiger! Once you become faithful to your time, you will find that you can write an extraordinary amount in fifteen minutes. You can pray or read inspirational material to assist you in decision-making matters of the day or encourage you to keep facing the challenges that this day will present. Fifteen minutes can go a long way.

D. Practice having personal-growth time for one year, and see how that changes your life, your attitude, your dreams, and your very soul. If a year feels too long, try it for a month and then for monthly increments: June, July, August, and so on.

E. This journal has also been reformatted for digital download. It follows a path from your childhood to the present. It is full of questions that are designed to help you evoke your thoughts and feelings and to assist you in developing this time just for you. May you enjoy your journey and delight in the self you find at the end of this journal. May you learn to trust yourself and be safe with yourself throughout this process. Please use it in any way that makes sense to you!

With many blessings for abundance and self-growth,
Robin B. Dilley, PhD

Tips on How to Use This Journal

1. Take advantage of personal-development and redirection time.

2. Write daily—take this journal with you or create a daily writing space.

3. Feel free to write as much or as little as you want. Feel free to skip questions, but just make sure you ask yourself, "What might come up if I answer the question I want to skip?" Feeling pages and journal tips are provided to help you stay motivated.

4. This journal is not intended to be finished in a week or even a month. Give yourself time to digest and explore the feelings that surface. There are enough exercises to take three months to complete. Take your time, but stay on task.

5. When you get to the end of the journal, you will find that you have come full circle. The exercises are designed to flow in consecutive order. Feel free to break the rules by finding the questions that speak to you in the now, and address those questions as desired. Enjoy your process.

And again, at the risk of being redundant, this journal is designed as an adjunctive tool to be used by people who want to begin or take the next step in their healing journey. But if a friend has given you this book or you picked it up from some other source, you may find that the questions bring up issues that you will want to work through with a trained professional.

The best way to find a good psychotherapist is to ask someone who is already seeing one, check with you family doctor, or reach out to your local American and Family Therapist or Licensed Psychological Associations. And again, remember: if you are not connecting within three sessions, keep looking. A bad therapeutic match can slow and damage your journey. May you enjoy this process, and may it be filled with blessings and self-growth.

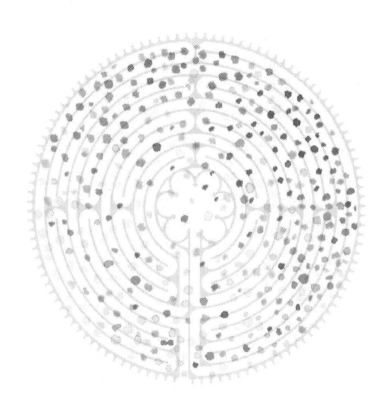

The Beginning

Staring at a blank page or writing a cold-call letter to yourself may feel hard, so please allow me to assist you in the process. This first letter will serve as a reminder to yourself as to why you are starting this journey.

Take a minute and close your eyes. Practice slow breathing before you begin. See how slowly you can breathe and how deeply you can take oxygen into your lungs. Let yourself imagine the oxygen feeding your cells, nourishing and massaging each individual cell in your body. Then allow your mind to drift back through the pages of your life. Imagine your life as a novel sitting in your lap; the last chapter is where you are today. Drift back through the pages of your novel by the decades. What has happened in the past ten years and the years prior? What was happening in your first ten years? As you visit the pages of your life, you may discover there are stirrings in your heart, emotions that come up. What would you say to yourself? Below on the page, just allow yourself to write to yourself what is in your heart today. What are your desires for yourself, your wishes, your regrets, your dreams? Let them flow as if you are writing your soul a love letter.

Use these next few lines to express what you are feeling now. This is a warm-up for the letter you will write on next page.

_____

_____

_____

_____

_____

_____

_____

_____

_____

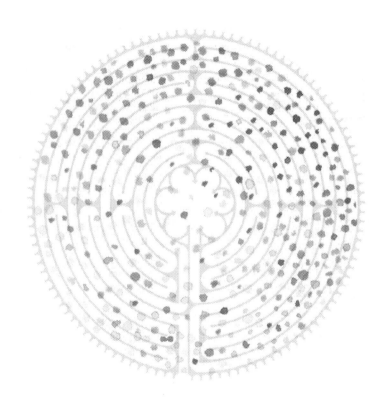

The Beginning

Date: / /

Dear Self,

(In this letter, allow yourself to talk to yourself, letting yourself weave in and out of what you want to say without letting the editor in your head be in control. You may find it helpful to tell yourself your life story up to this point, or you may want to fill the letter with your hopes and dreams. What do you want yourself to know about why you are starting this journey?)

_____
_____
_____
_____
_____
_____
_____
_____
_____
_____
_____
_____
_____
_____
_____
_____
_____
_____
_____
_____
_____
_____
_____
_____
_____
_____
_____
_____

Questions for Reflection and Introspection

The following exercises are questions. I am well aware some of you will write volumes and others will write paragraphs. So please use these questions as guidelines, and not mandates, to assist you as you weave through the pages of your life. If you need additional writing space, you can add blank pages.

1. If you had three wishes for this year, what would they be and why?

_____

_____

_____

_____

_____

_____

_____

_____

_____

_____

_____

_____

_____

_____

_____

_____

_____

_____

_____

_____

_____

_____

2. What do those three wishes reveal about you?

_____
_____
_____
_____
_____
_____
_____
_____
_____
_____
_____
_____
_____
_____
_____
_____
_____
_____
_____
_____
_____
_____
_____
_____
_____
_____
_____
_____
_____
_____
_____

3. Remember how magical it was when you were little and wished upon the first star of the night with such excitement? Who stole your magic of wishing upon a star when you were a little child? What events or people took that magic away?

_____

_____

_____

_____

_____

_____

_____

_____

_____

_____

_____

_____

_____

_____

_____

_____

_____

_____

_____

_____

_____

_____

_____

_____

_____

_____

_____

_____

_____

4. How can you retrieve the magic? Can you risk wishing upon that first star of the evening again?

_____

_____

_____

_____

_____

_____

_____

_____

_____

_____

_____

_____

_____

_____

_____

_____

_____

_____

_____

_____

_____

_____

_____

_____

_____

_____

_____

_____

_____

5. For question #1, you listed three wishes. The first one listed is ...

_____

_____

_____

_____

_____

_____

_____

_____

_____

_____

_____

_____

_____

_____

_____

_____

_____

_____

_____

_____

_____

_____

_____

_____

_____

_____

_____

_____

_____

_____

_____

_____

6. How would your life be different if that wish came true?

_____
_____
_____
_____
_____
_____
_____
_____
_____
_____
_____
_____
_____
_____
_____
_____
_____
_____
_____
_____
_____
_____
_____
_____
_____
_____
_____
_____
_____
_____
_____
_____

7. What can you do differently today to make it come true?

_____
_____
_____
_____
_____
_____
_____
_____
_____
_____
_____
_____
_____
_____
_____
_____
_____
_____
_____
_____
_____
_____
_____
_____
_____
_____
_____
_____
_____
_____

8. How does fear stop you from taking action?

_____

_____

_____

_____

_____

_____

_____

_____

_____

_____

_____

_____

_____

_____

_____

_____

_____

_____

_____

_____

_____

_____

_____

_____

_____

_____

_____

_____

_____

_____

_____

9. In order to not be afraid, what is one thing you must do differently?

_____

_____

_____

_____

_____

_____

_____

_____

_____

_____

_____

_____

_____

_____

_____

_____

_____

_____

_____

_____

_____

_____

_____

_____

_____

_____

_____

_____

_____

_____

_____

_____

10. What is fear?

11. If you accept your fear, how does it help you?

_____
_____
_____
_____
_____
_____
_____
_____
_____
_____
_____
_____
_____
_____
_____
_____
_____
_____
_____
_____
_____
_____
_____
_____
_____
_____
_____
_____
_____
_____
_____
_____

12. The last time you remember being really afraid was …

_____
_____
_____
_____
_____
_____
_____
_____
_____
_____
_____
_____
_____
_____
_____
_____
_____
_____
_____
_____
_____
_____
_____
_____
_____
_____
_____
_____
_____
_____
_____

13. What did you do? How did you react?

_____
_____
_____
_____
_____
_____
_____
_____
_____
_____
_____
_____
_____
_____
_____
_____
_____
_____
_____
_____
_____
_____
_____
_____
_____
_____
_____
_____
_____
_____
_____
_____

14. What do you wish you had done instead?

_____
_____
_____
_____
_____
_____
_____
_____
_____
_____
_____
_____
_____
_____
_____
_____
_____
_____
_____
_____
_____
_____
_____
_____
_____
_____
_____
_____
_____
_____
_____

15. How can you make it different for yourself in the future?

_____

_____

_____

_____

_____

_____

_____

_____

_____

_____

_____

_____

_____

_____

_____

_____

_____

_____

_____

_____

_____

_____

_____

_____

_____

_____

_____

_____

16. What commitment or action must you take to address your fear and overcome or befriend it?

_____

_____

_____

_____

_____

_____

_____

_____

_____

_____

_____

_____

_____

_____

_____

_____

_____

_____

_____

_____

_____

_____

_____

_____

_____

_____

_____

_____

17. How would your life be different if you overcame your fear?

_____
_____
_____
_____
_____
_____
_____
_____
_____
_____
_____
_____
_____
_____
_____
_____
_____
_____
_____
_____
_____
_____
_____
_____
_____
_____
_____
_____
_____

18. If your life *were* different, what challenges would leaving the safety net of the familiar create?

_____

_____

_____

_____

_____

_____

_____

_____

_____

_____

_____

_____

_____

_____

_____

_____

_____

_____

_____

_____

_____

_____

_____

_____

_____

_____

_____

_____

_____

An Exercise in Creativity

Often, the simple act of externalizing your emotions can help address the issues surrounding them. Art therapy is a great way to do this. The good news is you do not have to be an artist; all you need are some crayons, colored pencils, or magic markers (a pen or pencil will also work).

Art is an exceptional way to enter your internal space. Something as simple as doodling with a crayon without thinking will take you to feelings not easily articulated. Choose colors that speak about your fear, and let the colors express themselves on this page. After you are finished, date and title your piece of emotional art.

Color Your Feelings Here

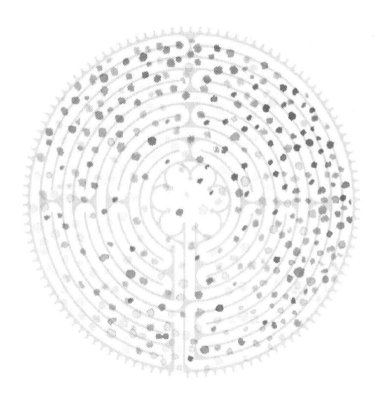

Other Feelings Worth Exploring

By now you might be saying, "I'm tired of focusing on fear. What feeling can I explore next?" Good question! Write down all the other feelings you've encountered while working on fear, and then circle some new feelings to explore. Below is a list of feelings to help you get started.

_____
_____
_____
_____
_____
_____
_____
_____

Accepted	Confused	Enthusiastic
Afraid	Concerned	Envious
Annoyed	Defeated	Ecstatic
Anxious	Defensive	Excited
Angry	Depressed	Fearful
Ashamed	Detached	Foolish
Bashful	Disappointed	Free
Bewildered	Disgusted	Frustrated
Bitter	Distracted	Furious
Bored	Disturbed	Glum
Brave	Eager	Good
Calm	Edgy	Guilty
Confident	Embarrassed	Happy

Helpless
High
Hopeful
Hostile
Humiliated
Hurt
Inadequate
Inhibited
Intense
Intimidated
Irritable
Jazzed
Jealous
Joyful

Lonely
Loving
Mean
Miserable
Needed
Neglected
Nervous
Passionate
Peaceful
Pessimistic
Playful
Pleased
Pressured
Protective

Puzzled
Rejected
Relieved
Resentful
Restless
Sad
Safe
Sensual
Sentimental
Sexual
Sexy
Shaky
Shy

Which feeling did you choose to explore? What drew you toward that feeling?

_____

_____

_____

_____

_____

_____

_____

_____

_____

_____

_____

_____

_____

_____

_____

_____

_____

_____

_____

_____

_____

_____

_____

_____

_____

_____

_____

_____

_____

_____

_____

_____

Going Deeper with that Feeling

1. When was the last time you had this feeling? What did you do with it? Or what did it do for you?

_____

_____

_____

_____

_____

_____

_____

_____

_____

_____

_____

_____

_____

_____

_____

_____

_____

_____

_____

_____

_____

2. By answering the question above, how does this feeling serve you now?

_____

_____

_____

_____

_____

_____

_____

_____

_____

_____

_____

_____

_____

_____

_____

_____

_____

_____

_____

_____

_____

_____

_____

_____

_____

_____

_____

_____

_____

_____

_____

_____

_____

3. What is the benefit you gain when you bring along this feeling?

_____

_____

_____

_____

_____

_____

_____

_____

_____

_____

_____

_____

_____

_____

_____

_____

_____

_____

_____

_____

_____

_____

_____

_____

_____

_____

_____

_____

_____

_____

_____

_____

4. When was the first time you remember having this feeling?

_____
_____
_____
_____
_____
_____
_____
_____
_____
_____
_____
_____
_____
_____
_____
_____
_____
_____
_____
_____
_____
_____
_____
_____
_____
_____
_____
_____
_____
_____
_____

5. What did you learn from your mother about the feeling you selected?

_____
_____
_____
_____
_____
_____
_____
_____
_____
_____
_____
_____
_____
_____
_____
_____
_____
_____
_____
_____
_____
_____
_____
_____
_____
_____
_____
_____
_____
_____
_____

6. What did you learn from your father about this same feeling?

_____

_____

_____

_____

_____

_____

_____

_____

_____

_____

_____

_____

_____

_____

_____

_____

_____

_____

_____

_____

_____

_____

_____

_____

_____

_____

_____

_____

_____

7. By answering the above questions, are you beginning to see how your family system still influences your adult life?

_____
_____
_____
_____
_____
_____
_____
_____
_____
_____
_____
_____
_____
_____
_____
_____
_____
_____
_____
_____
_____
_____
_____
_____
_____
_____
_____
_____
_____
_____
_____

8. How many ways do you think the family you grew up in still affects you today?

___

9. Would you like to get rid of those patterns created in your childhood? Spend some time writing about the patterns you want to change. Identifying and naming the pattern will help you create an action plan. For instance, If you avoid people you are angry with rather than having a conversation with them, then write about why you avoid them. When did you start using avoiding behavior and how is not working for you?

_____

_____

_____

_____

_____

_____

_____

_____

_____

_____

_____

_____

_____

_____

_____

_____

_____

_____

_____

_____

_____

_____

_____

_____

10. That means changing. Are you up to it?

_____

_____

_____

_____

_____

_____

_____

_____

_____

_____

_____

_____

_____

_____

_____

_____

_____

_____

_____

_____

_____

_____

_____

_____

_____

_____

11. If you change, what will you have to give up? Dig deep.

_____
_____
_____
_____
_____
_____
_____
_____
_____
_____
_____
_____
_____
_____
_____
_____
_____
_____
_____
_____
_____
_____
_____
_____
_____
_____
_____
_____
_____
_____
_____
_____

12. If you change, how will you be different?

_____

_____

_____

_____

_____

_____

_____

_____

_____

_____

_____

_____

_____

_____

_____

_____

_____

_____

_____

_____

_____

_____

_____

_____

_____

_____

_____

_____

_____

_____

_____

_____

_____

13. What is frightening about being different from before?

_____

_____

_____

_____

_____

_____

_____

_____

_____

_____

_____

_____

_____

_____

_____

_____

_____

_____

_____

_____

_____

_____

_____

_____

_____

_____

_____

_____

_____

_____

_____

14. Who won't like you if you change? And how does that make you feel?

_____

_____

_____

_____

_____

_____

_____

_____

_____

_____

_____

_____

_____

_____

_____

_____

_____

_____

_____

_____

_____

_____

_____

_____

_____

_____

_____

_____

_____

_____

Genogram the Psychodrama Way

(Choose an age, such as four, eight, ten, etc., from which to answer the following questions.)

First, choose two words to describe yourself at that age. What type of child were you?

_____

_____

_____

_____

   A. Choose two words to describe your father's personality.

_____

_____

_____

_____

   B. Choose two words to describe your mother's personality.

_____

_____

_____

_____

   C. Choose two words to describe each of your siblings (brothers, sisters).

_____

_____

_____

_____

D. Choose two words to describe your parents' marital relationship.

_____

_____

_____

_____

E. Choose two words to describe the relationship you had with each family member.

_____

_____

_____

_____

F. Describe each of your grandparents using two words. Next, choose two words would your parents choose to describe them? How are the descriptions different from each other?

_____

_____

_____

G. Who is the family hero? (The hero is the person in your family who seems to always get praise regardless of what they do.) How do you feel when you are around that person?

_____

_____

_____

H. Who is the family scapegoat? (The person who is always talked about and who seems to always have chaos and problems in his/her life?) How do you feel about him/her?

_____

_____

_____

I. Who were the heroes and scapegoats among your parents' siblings (your aunts and uncles)?

_____
_____
_____
_____
_____
_____
_____
_____
_____
_____
_____
_____
_____
_____
_____
_____
_____
_____
_____
_____
_____
_____
_____
_____
_____
_____
_____
_____
_____

J. In one sentence, sum up the message, spoken or unspoken, that your mother had for you when you were a child. How would that message be different now?

_____
_____
_____
_____
_____
_____
_____
_____
_____
_____
_____
_____
_____
_____
_____
_____
_____
_____
_____
_____
_____
_____
_____
_____
_____
_____
_____
_____
_____
_____
_____
_____

K. Repeat question "J" describing each of your family members.

L. Now, go through the above questions "J" and "K" and answer them from the perspective of your present age.

_____
_____
_____
_____
_____
_____
_____
_____
_____
_____
_____
_____
_____
_____
_____
_____
_____
_____
_____
_____
_____
_____
_____
_____
_____
_____
_____
_____
_____
_____

M. Repeat the same exercise with your nuclear family (partner and children).

If you do not have a nuclear family you can choose from your friends or colleagues to explore your choices of people in your life. You can also use the following pages to delve deeper into your current feelings.

_____

_____

_____

_____

_____

_____

_____

_____

_____

_____

_____

_____

_____

_____

_____

_____

_____

_____

_____

_____

_____

N. List each of their messages to you.

_____
_____
_____
_____
_____
_____
_____
_____
_____
_____
_____
_____
_____
_____
_____
_____
_____
_____
_____
_____
_____
_____
_____
_____
_____
_____
_____
_____
_____

O. How are the messages the same and how are they different from the ones you received as a child?

_____

_____

_____

_____

_____

_____

_____

_____

_____

_____

_____

_____

_____

_____

_____

_____

_____

_____

_____

_____

_____

_____

_____

_____

_____

_____

_____

_____

_____

_____

If you have other children what are his/her traits like?

P. Which child is most like your mother? Which is most like your father?

_____
_____
_____
_____

Q.

_____
_____
_____
_____

What other traits do you recognize about your children. Which one is the family hero?
_____

Which child is the family scapegoat?
_____
_____
_____
_____
_____
_____
_____
_____
_____
_____
_____
_____
_____
_____

R. Draw a picture of your family of origin having dinner.

S. Draw a picture of your nuclear family (spouse and children) having dinner.

If you do not have a nuclear family draw a picture of the people in your life now. Draw another picture of how you want your extended family (friends and colleagues) to look.

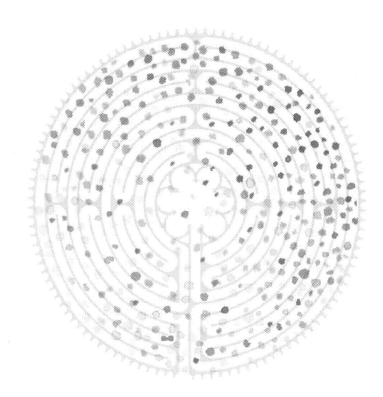

T. If you could change one thing about your family of origin what would it be? Why? List all of what you want to be different. Go for everything you ever wanted.

_____
_____
_____
_____
_____
_____
_____
_____
_____
_____
_____
_____
_____
_____
_____
_____
_____
_____
_____
_____
_____
_____
_____
_____
_____
_____
_____
_____

U. If you could change one thing about your nuclear family (spouse, children, friends or colleagues) what would it be? Again go for how you would like your life to be now. Write your wildest fantasy.

_____

_____

_____

_____

_____

_____

_____

_____

_____

_____

_____

_____

_____

_____

_____

_____

_____

_____

_____

_____

_____

_____

_____

_____

_____

_____

_____

Further Family-of-Origin Exploration

1. When you filled out "U" on previous page, what feelings came rising into your awareness?

_____
_____
_____
_____
_____
_____
_____
_____
_____
_____
_____
_____
_____
_____
_____
_____
_____
_____
_____
_____
_____

2. How do you see your mother and father's personality traits in yourself?

_____

_____

_____

_____

_____

_____

_____

_____

_____

_____

_____

_____

_____

_____

_____

_____

_____

_____

_____

_____

_____

_____

_____

_____

_____

_____

_____

_____

3. Which two words would you use to describe yourself?

_____

_____

_____

_____

4. Do you want to change those traits or keep them? Why?

_____

_____

_____

_____

_____

_____

_____

_____

_____

_____

_____

_____

_____

_____

_____

_____

_____

_____

_____

_____

_____

_____

5. Which messages from the genogram exercise offer you hope? If none of them, then how do you get your hope now?

_____
_____
_____
_____
_____
_____
_____
_____
_____
_____
_____
_____
_____
_____
_____
_____
_____
_____
_____
_____
_____
_____
_____
_____
_____
_____
_____
_____
_____
_____
_____

6. What is hope?

7. Who stole your mother's hope? How?

8. Who stole your father's hope? How?

9. Are you angry or sad right now? Write about it.

_____
_____
_____
_____
_____
_____
_____
_____
_____
_____
_____
_____
_____
_____
_____
_____
_____
_____
_____
_____
_____
_____
_____
_____
_____
_____
_____
_____
_____
_____
_____

10. What were the rules about anger, spoken and unspoken, in your household growing up?

_____

_____

_____

_____

_____

_____

_____

_____

_____

_____

_____

_____

_____

_____

_____

_____

_____

_____

_____

_____

_____

_____

_____

_____

_____

_____

_____

_____

11. What did you do with your anger as a child?

_____
_____
_____
_____
_____
_____
_____
_____
_____
_____
_____
_____
_____
_____
_____
_____
_____
_____
_____
_____
_____
_____
_____
_____
_____
_____
_____
_____
_____
_____

12. What happened when you became angry?

_____
_____
_____
_____
_____
_____
_____
_____
_____
_____
_____
_____
_____
_____
_____
_____
_____
_____
_____
_____
_____
_____
_____
_____
_____
_____
_____
_____
_____

13. What types of situations or circumstances in your family made you angry?

_____

_____

_____

_____

_____

_____

_____

_____

_____

_____

_____

_____

_____

_____

_____

_____

_____

_____

_____

_____

_____

_____

_____

_____

_____

_____

_____

_____

_____

_____

14. How did you know when your mother was angry? What did she do? What did you do when your mother was angry?

_____

_____

_____

_____

_____

_____

_____

_____

_____

_____

_____

_____

_____

_____

_____

_____

_____

_____

_____

_____

_____

_____

_____

_____

_____

_____

_____

_____

_____

15. How did you know when your father was angry? What did he do? What did you do when your father was angry?

_____

_____

_____

_____

_____

_____

_____

_____

_____

_____

_____

_____

_____

_____

_____

_____

_____

_____

_____

_____

_____

_____

_____

_____

_____

_____

_____

_____

_____

16. How do you wish your parents had comforted you when they were angry?

_____
_____
_____
_____
_____
_____
_____
_____
_____
_____
_____
_____
_____
_____
_____
_____
_____
_____
_____
_____
_____
_____
_____
_____
_____
_____
_____
_____
_____
_____

17. What comforting words did you long to hear?

_____

_____

_____

_____

_____

_____

_____

_____

_____

_____

_____

_____

_____

_____

_____

_____

_____

_____

_____

_____

_____

_____

_____

_____

_____

_____

_____

18. How would you have liked that comfort to look? How can your creativity and imagination give yourself that comfort now? Write how you would comfort your inner child today if your parents were angry.

_____
_____
_____
_____
_____
_____
_____
_____
_____
_____
_____
_____
_____
_____
_____
_____
_____
_____
_____
_____
_____
_____
_____
_____
_____
_____

19. What types of things make you angry now?

_____
_____
_____
_____
_____
_____
_____
_____
_____
_____
_____
_____
_____
_____
_____
_____
_____
_____
_____
_____
_____
_____
_____
_____
_____
_____
_____
_____
_____

20. When were you last angry? What did you do with the anger?

_____
_____
_____
_____
_____
_____
_____
_____
_____
_____
_____
_____
_____
_____
_____
_____
_____
_____
_____
_____
_____
_____
_____
_____
_____
_____

21. How do you wish you had handled your anger differently, if at all?

_____

_____

_____

_____

_____

_____

_____

_____

_____

_____

_____

_____

_____

_____

_____

_____

_____

_____

_____

_____

_____

_____

_____

_____

_____

_____

_____

_____

_____

_____

_____

22. How can you do things differently next time?

_____

_____

_____

_____

_____

_____

_____

_____

_____

_____

_____

_____

_____

_____

_____

_____

_____

_____

_____

_____

_____

_____

_____

_____

_____

_____

_____

_____

_____

23. How does your anger make you feel powerful?

_____

_____

_____

_____

_____

_____

_____

_____

_____

_____

_____

_____

_____

_____

_____

_____

_____

_____

_____

_____

_____

_____

_____

_____

_____

_____

_____

_____

24. How do you feel and behave when you feel powerful?

_____
_____
_____
_____
_____
_____
_____
_____
_____
_____
_____
_____
_____
_____
_____
_____
_____
_____
_____
_____
_____
_____
_____
_____
_____
_____
_____
_____
_____

25. Who is the most powerful person you know? Why?

_____
_____
_____
_____
_____
_____
_____
_____
_____
_____
_____
_____
_____
_____
_____
_____
_____
_____
_____
_____
_____
_____
_____
_____
_____
_____
_____
_____

26. Do you like and feel safe around their power? If so, how does their power help you feel safe?

_____

_____

_____

_____

_____

_____

_____

_____

_____

_____

_____

_____

_____

_____

_____

_____

_____

_____

_____

_____

_____

_____

_____

_____

_____

_____

_____

_____

_____

27. If you were to ask them (in your imagination or in person) how they could help you learn to explore your own power, what would they tell you?

_____
_____
_____
_____
_____
_____
_____
_____
_____
_____
_____
_____
_____
_____
_____
_____
_____
_____
_____
_____
_____
_____
_____
_____
_____
_____
_____
_____
_____
_____
_____

28. What did your mother teach you about personal power?

_____

_____

_____

_____

_____

_____

_____

_____

_____

_____

_____

_____

_____

_____

_____

_____

_____

_____

_____

_____

_____

_____

_____

_____

_____

_____

_____

_____

_____

29. Do you feel shame when you feel good about yourself? If yes, what do you find yourself thinking?

_____

_____

_____

_____

_____

_____

_____

_____

_____

_____

_____

_____

_____

_____

_____

_____

_____

_____

_____

_____

_____

_____

_____

_____

_____

_____

30. When you look back at your mother's use of power, what do you remember? How do you feel about her? Do you think she was weak or did you learn to respect her because of her power?

_____
_____
_____
_____
_____
_____
_____
_____
_____
_____
_____
_____
_____
_____
_____
_____
_____
_____
_____
_____
_____
_____
_____
_____
_____
_____
_____

31. What about your dad's power? What did he teach you about the quality of power and how do you feel about it?

_____

_____

_____

_____

_____

_____

_____

_____

_____

_____

_____

_____

_____

_____

_____

_____

_____

_____

_____

_____

_____

_____

_____

_____

_____

_____

_____

_____

32. If you were to ask your parents (in your imagination or in person) how they could help you learn to explore your own power, what would they tell you?

_____

_____

_____

_____

_____

_____

_____

_____

_____

_____

_____

_____

_____

_____

_____

_____

_____

_____

_____

_____

_____

_____

_____

_____

_____

_____

_____

_____

_____

33. How does your anger make you feel helpless?

_____
_____
_____
_____
_____
_____
_____
_____
_____
_____
_____
_____
_____
_____
_____
_____
_____
_____
_____
_____
_____
_____
_____
_____
_____
_____
_____
_____
_____
_____

34. How do you behave when you feel helpless?

_____
_____
_____
_____
_____
_____
_____
_____
_____
_____
_____
_____
_____
_____
_____
_____
_____
_____
_____
_____
_____
_____
_____
_____
_____
_____
_____
_____

35. When your anger makes you feel helpless, what can you do instead?

_____

_____

_____

_____

_____

_____

_____

_____

_____

_____

_____

_____

_____

_____

_____

_____

_____

_____

_____

_____

_____

_____

_____

_____

_____

_____

_____

_____

36. What other feelings make you feel helpless?

_____
_____
_____
_____
_____
_____
_____
_____
_____
_____
_____
_____
_____
_____
_____
_____
_____
_____
_____
_____
_____
_____
_____
_____
_____
_____
_____
_____
_____
_____
_____
_____

37. What is helplessness and how does it overtake you?

38. Look at the next page on Personification and choose something in your present visual surroundings to personify helplessness. Write about it. For example, "I am this helpless empty vase. Once upon a time, I held beautiful flowers, but not anymore! Why won't anyone pay attention to me?"

_____

_____

_____

_____

_____

_____

_____

_____

_____

_____

_____

_____

_____

_____

_____

_____

_____

_____

_____

_____

_____

_____

_____

_____

_____

_____

Creative Journaling through Personification

Personification means to think of an object as if it has life and human qualities. To use personification as a writer means to allow your creative mind to freely wander, placing feelings, dreams, desires, and situations onto an object. This is a great tool for helping yourself get beyond the mundane qualities of your daily writing and create something totally from projection. Below are some tips to help you.

A. Write in first person, present tense.

B. Choose an object in your visual surroundings—for instance, your coffee cup.

C. Spend a moment thinking about the object. Pick it up and look at it. Touch the texture of the object. Smell it. How would the object taste if all of those colors and textures turned into taste? Empathize with the object. What is it feeling? How was the object born? Did the object like the family into which it was born? How did the object come to live with you?

_____

_____

_____

_____

_____

_____

_____

_____

_____

_____

_____

_____

D. How did it catch your attention now? What does the object want to tell you? Does it have a special story, a pain, a fear, a sadness it wants you to hear?

_____

_____

_____

_____

_____

_____

_____

_____

_____

_____

_____

_____

_____

_____

_____

_____

_____

_____

_____

_____

_____

_____

_____

_____

_____

_____

_____

_____

E. Write the object's story. For instance, "I am a coffee cup. I am quite beautifully created out of beautiful blue, mauve, and earth tones. My creator is quite proud of me because he is of the Koskimo tribe in the Northwest. His ancestry runs deep. My creator comes from a proud people, but a people who have great pain, great sadness … I felt his sadness and his heart as he placed me on the potter's wheel. My creator was very kind and gentle with me." See how easily the story begins to unfold. Let yourself explore this process by writing two to three pages. Or you can do a timed writing for ten to fifteen minutes. When you finish your personification, you can stop or you can add any of the below to your writing from the object's point-of-view.

A. I wish …	E. I can …	I. I hope for …
B. I know …	F. I see …	J. I know …
C. I would like to do …	G. I can't …	K. I would like to
D. I like …	H. I want …	know if …
L. I would like for you to …		

Leave the writing when you are finished. Reread it later and explore the feelings this writing brings up for you. Write those feelings down.

_____

_____

_____

_____

_____

_____

_____

_____

_____

_____

_____

_____

_____

_____

_____

Color your Helplessness

Externalize your helplessness as you did with your fear. What does it look like? Or just abstractly color the feelings your helplessness brings up for you. Finish by naming and dating your masterpiece.

The BIG T: Trust

Return to the Genogram Section, page 75, and review the answers to your questions. Use your reflections to move toward these next questions about trust.

1. What were the rules about trust in your family?

_____

_____

_____

_____

_____

_____

_____

_____

_____

_____

_____

_____

_____

2. What did you learn about trust from your family?

_____

_____

_____

_____

_____

_____

_____

_____

_____

_____

_____

_____

3. What did your father teach you about trust? Could you trust him? How did you know whether you could or could not trust him?

_____

_____

_____

_____

_____

_____

_____

_____

_____

_____

_____

_____

4. What did you do about your trust or mistrust with your father?

_____

_____

_____

_____

_____

_____

_____

_____

_____

_____

5. How about your mother? Did you trust her? How did she earn or not earn your trust?

_____

_____

_____

_____

_____

_____

_____

_____

_____

_____

_____

6. What do you think your mother learned about trust in her family when she was growing up?

_____

_____

_____

_____

_____

_____

_____

_____

_____

_____

_____

7. Did your mother and father trust each other? How did you know?

_____

_____

_____

_____

_____

_____

_____

_____

_____

_____

_____

8. What did you do about your trust or mistrust with your mother?

_____

_____

_____

_____

_____

_____

_____

_____

_____

_____

_____

9. Did you trust your siblings? Which ones did you trust the least? Which ones the most? Why?

_____

_____

_____

_____

_____

_____

_____

_____

_____

_____

10. Could your siblings trust you? How do you know that they could or could not trust you?

_____

_____

_____

_____

_____

_____

_____

_____

_____

_____

11. What is your most painful memory about a time when your trust was shattered?

_____

_____

_____

_____

_____

_____

_____

_____

_____

_____

_____

_____

_____

_____

_____

_____

_____

_____

_____

_____

_____

_____

_____

_____

_____

_____

_____

_____

12. What behavior did you develop to protect yourself from the shattering of your trust?

_____

_____

_____

_____

_____

_____

_____

_____

_____

_____

_____

_____

_____

_____

_____

_____

_____

_____

_____

_____

_____

_____

_____

_____

_____

_____

_____

_____

_____

13. How does that behavior prevent you from enjoying the love of others now?

_____

_____

_____

_____

_____

_____

_____

_____

_____

_____

_____

_____

_____

_____

_____

_____

_____

_____

_____

_____

_____

_____

_____

_____

_____

_____

_____

_____

_____

_____

_____

14. How would you like to change or open up your heart and allow trust to grow again in your life?

_____

_____

_____

_____

_____

_____

_____

_____

_____

_____

_____

_____

_____

_____

_____

_____

_____

_____

_____

_____

_____

_____

_____

_____

_____

15. Whom do you trust now and why?

_____
_____
_____
_____
_____
_____
_____
_____
_____
_____
_____
_____
_____
_____
_____
_____
_____
_____
_____
_____
_____
_____
_____
_____
_____
_____
_____

16. What makes that person(s) safe to trust? How do you know?

_____

_____

_____

_____

_____

_____

_____

_____

_____

_____

_____

_____

_____

_____

_____

_____

_____

_____

_____

_____

_____

_____

_____

_____

_____

_____

_____

_____

_____

_____

_____

_____

17. How can you use protection in a positive way instead of a defensive way in order to trust and stay safe at the same time?

_____

_____

_____

_____

_____

_____

_____

_____

_____

_____

_____

_____

_____

_____

_____

_____

_____

_____

_____

_____

_____

_____

_____

_____

_____

_____

_____

_____

_____

_____

The BIG S: Spirituality

1. What does trust have to do with spirituality?

2. What is spirituality?

_____

_____

_____

_____

_____

_____

_____

_____

_____

_____

_____

_____

_____

_____

_____

_____

_____

_____

_____

_____

_____

_____

_____

_____

_____

_____

_____

_____

_____

_____

3. How do you practice spirituality?

_____

_____

_____

_____

_____

_____

_____

_____

_____

_____

_____

_____

_____

_____

_____

_____

_____

_____

_____

_____

_____

_____

_____

_____

_____

_____

_____

4. What was your family's picture of God? How did they let you know their God?

_____
_____
_____
_____
_____
_____
_____
_____
_____
_____
_____
_____
_____
_____
_____
_____
_____
_____
_____
_____
_____
_____
_____
_____
_____
_____
_____
_____
_____
_____
_____
_____
_____
_____

5. Because of what you learned about God from your family, what feelings do you have about God?

_____

_____

_____

_____

_____

_____

_____

_____

_____

_____

_____

_____

_____

_____

_____

_____

_____

_____

_____

_____

_____

_____

_____

_____

_____

_____

_____

_____

_____

6. What did your mother's family teach you about spirituality or God?

_____

_____

_____

_____

_____

_____

_____

_____

_____

_____

_____

_____

_____

_____

_____

_____

_____

_____

_____

_____

_____

_____

_____

_____

_____

_____

_____

_____

_____

_____

_____

_____

7. What did your father's family teach you about spirituality or God?

_____

_____

_____

_____

_____

_____

_____

_____

_____

_____

_____

_____

_____

_____

_____

_____

_____

_____

_____

_____

_____

_____

_____

_____

_____

_____

_____

_____

_____

_____

8. What would you like to teach them about the God you know or want to know today?

_____

_____

_____

_____

_____

_____

_____

_____

_____

_____

_____

_____

_____

_____

_____

_____

_____

_____

_____

_____

_____

_____

_____

_____

_____

_____

_____

9. Write God a letter about what it was like growing up in your family. Tell God how your image of spirituality was affected as a result of the stories, behavior, and rules your family set in place about religion and faith.

_____

_____

_____

_____

_____

_____

_____

_____

_____

_____

_____

_____

_____

_____

_____

_____

_____

_____

_____

_____

_____

_____

_____

_____

_____

_____

_____

_____

_____

10. Try writing a response from God to that child who learned what he/she did in his/her family about spirituality and faith.

_____
_____
_____
_____
_____
_____
_____
_____
_____
_____
_____
_____
_____
_____
_____
_____
_____
_____
_____
_____
_____
_____
_____
_____
_____
_____
_____
_____
_____
_____
_____

11. Design your spiritual path for the next couple of weeks or months. What do you want it to look like? How will you set aside time in your busy life to practice spirituality? What ingredients will you make sure are a part of your spiritual path? (Empathy, compassion, prayer, giving, serving, reading, writing, meditation, exercise—there are so many options! Take a few minutes to think, reflect, and pray. Then write your next spiritual step below.

Color a Personal Prayer for Yourself

Allow yourself to choose three to five different colors and just move the crayons around on the paper in a prayerful/mindful way as you think about what it is you want/need to say to some power greater than yourself. Just notice what happens inside as you do this without using words.

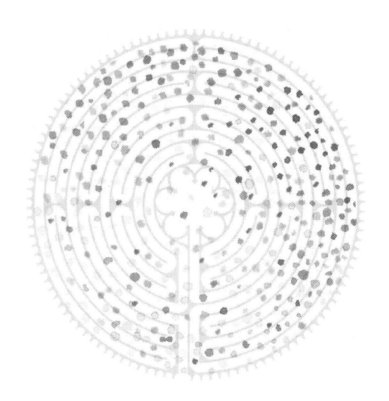

You: Your Body Image

We have explored some powerful feelings of fear, helplessness, trust, and spirituality. Now it is time to look at how you view your body and all of the messages you have acquired about your body throughout your life. I am aware some of you are now experiencing dread and are perhaps a bit nauseated as I bring the word "body" to the foreground. Your body needs you as much as the little child within you needs you. No one else is going to care about your body if you do not take care of it. When you mistreat it, you are replicating the bad and hurtful things that happened to you in your past. Please breathe into these exercises and allow yourself the opportunity to love yourself at a deeper level than you ever thought you could.

1. Let's start with the positive. What do you like about the way you look? Make yourself choose at least three things. (It could be the shape of your eyes, the color of your skin, the way your body looks in a favorite color, etc.)

_____

_____

_____

_____

_____

_____

_____

_____

_____

_____

_____

_____

2. When thinking of your body, what are you the most critical about and why?

_____

_____

_____

_____

_____

_____

_____

_____

_____

_____

_____

_____

_____

_____

_____

_____

_____

_____

_____

_____

_____

_____

_____

_____

_____

_____

_____

_____

_____

_____

_____

_____

3. How do you feel good about yourself and celebrate your body if you are always criticizing yourself? No, you did not misunderstand the question. You must change your negative messages if you want to change your relationship to your body. How can you celebrate your body?

_____

_____

_____

_____

_____

_____

_____

_____

_____

_____

_____

_____

_____

_____

_____

_____

_____

_____

_____

_____

_____

_____

_____

_____

_____

_____

_____

_____

4. You and your body have a very intimate connection. You carry it with you wherever you go! But I know from the work that I do that most people complain chronically about their body (their looks, nose, hips, weight, eyes, hair, etc.). I have yet to find someone who tells me that he/she absolutely loves his or her body. It is hard to override the cultural messages, but if you want to stop being a victim, you must find a way. As long as you let yourself be dictated to by the outside messages, you will be unhappy about the body you carry wherever you go. So before you write letters to your parents about the messages they gave you about your body, first, write an angry letter to the advertising industry. If you need to stir your anger a bit, spend this week looking at ads and commercials. Once you see that only "perfect" men and women are portrayed in these ads, let your anger rip. You are being abused and emotionally harassed by those commercials. It is as severe as child abuse, poverty, sexual harassment, gender biases, and other types of injustices in the world. Take a stand in your letter against these body-shaming advertisements.

_____

_____

_____

_____

_____

_____

_____

_____

_____

_____

_____

_____

_____

_____

_____

_____

_____

_____

_____

_____

5. Now that you have some anger off your chest about the culturally permissible sexual harassment issues, it is time to examine how you allow yourself to be seduced into their web of fantasy. What are the earliest messages you remember about your body? List them, and make yourself list at least fifteen of them. For instance, "Your teeth are crooked. You are too tall, too short, too broad-shouldered for a girl. You are too small for a boy. Your hair is a mess. You are too pudgy. You are too skinny." Identify the person(s) who gave those messages to you.

_____

_____

_____

_____

_____

_____

_____

_____

_____

_____

_____

_____

_____

_____

_____

_____

_____

_____

_____

_____

_____

_____

_____

_____

_____

_____

6. Think about those messages and the people that gave them to you. Choose one of them, perhaps the one that was/is the most painful for you to remember. Write your feelings about that message.

_____

_____

_____

_____

_____

_____

_____

_____

_____

_____

_____

_____

_____

_____

_____

_____

_____

_____

_____

_____

_____

_____

_____

_____

_____

_____

_____

_____

_____

_____

7. Now, spend a few quiet moments visiting in your mind's eye the person who gave you the negative message and write him/her a letter explaining how that message has hurt you up until now, but that you are going to overcome the lie and move toward accepting and loving your body just the way it is.

_____

_____

_____

_____

_____

_____

_____

_____

_____

_____

_____

_____

_____

_____

_____

_____

_____

_____

_____

_____

_____

_____

_____

_____

_____

_____

_____

_____

_____

8. Create a power symbol to carry with you for the next month as a reminder that you are taking your power back and giving the shame back to the person who gave it to you.

_____

_____

_____

_____

_____

_____

_____

_____

_____

_____

_____

_____

_____

_____

_____

_____

_____

_____

_____

_____

_____

_____

_____

_____

_____

_____

_____

_____

_____

_____

9. Which part of your body is the most difficult for you to accept now? Why? What do you tell yourself about it?

_____

_____

_____

_____

_____

_____

_____

_____

_____

_____

_____

_____

_____

_____

_____

_____

_____

_____

_____

_____

_____

_____

_____

_____

_____

_____

_____

_____

_____

_____

10. How would you like for it to be different? What will you have to do to make it so? How committed to the process are you?

_____

_____

_____

_____

_____

_____

_____

_____

_____

_____

_____

_____

_____

_____

_____

_____

_____

_____

_____

_____

_____

_____

_____

_____

_____

_____

_____

_____

_____

_____

_____

_____

11. What gets in the way of the commitment every time? What is that about?

_____

_____

_____

_____

_____

_____

_____

_____

_____

_____

_____

_____

_____

_____

_____

_____

_____

_____

_____

_____

_____

_____

_____

_____

_____

_____

_____

_____

_____

_____

_____

_____

12. Before we move on from the body section, let's take a look at your relationship with food. We could spend all sorts of time talking about your comfort foods and how much you use them to feed your emotional challenges, but I would rather leave this section on a positive note. What are the things that you are presently doing right about your eating habits?

_____
_____
_____
_____
_____
_____
_____
_____
_____
_____
_____
_____
_____
_____
_____
_____
_____
_____
_____
_____
_____
_____
_____
_____
_____
_____

13. How would you like to increase your effectiveness by doing more positive things about your eating habits? What can you do to strengthen and support those positive eating patterns now? After you make a list, write a letter of praise and support to yourself to continue with your good habits around food.

_____

_____

_____

_____

_____

_____

_____

_____

_____

_____

_____

_____

_____

_____

_____

_____

_____

_____

_____

_____

_____

_____

_____

_____

_____

_____

_____

_____

Coming Full Circle

I hope that as you have written putting the pieces of your family history and present life together in story form, you are beginning to open up and feel better about your past. Now that you are an adult it is up to you to change and create the life you want to live.

After Dorothy's adventure in OZ, she was changed by her experience. However, everyone else in the story remained the same. From this point forward, focus on what you can change and empower yourself to reach your dreams and wishes.

1. Where are you with your three wishes? You did some writing about your first wish. How is it coming along? Have you made it come true yet? If so, how? If not, what is the next step toward making it come true?

_____

_____

_____

_____

_____

_____

_____

_____

_____

_____

_____

_____

_____

_____

2. What do you need to do differently in order to keep working at wish number one?

_____

_____

_____

_____

_____

_____

_____

_____

_____

_____

_____

_____

_____

_____

_____

_____

_____

_____

_____

_____

_____

_____

_____

_____

_____

_____

_____

_____

_____

3. What gets in the way of the commitment every time? What is that about?

_____

_____

_____

_____

_____

_____

_____

_____

_____

_____

_____

_____

_____

_____

_____

_____

_____

_____

_____

_____

_____

_____

_____

_____

_____

_____

_____

_____

4. What is wish number two? Write it out. Do you still want it or do you want to change it?

_____

_____

_____

_____

_____

_____

_____

_____

_____

_____

_____

_____

_____

_____

_____

_____

_____

_____

_____

_____

_____

_____

_____

_____

_____

_____

_____

_____

5. If wish number two became true, how would your life be different? (Write that first.) Then answer this question: What do I need to do differently to make that happen?

_____

_____

_____

_____

_____

_____

_____

_____

_____

_____

_____

_____

_____

_____

_____

_____

_____

_____

_____

_____

_____

_____

_____

_____

_____

6. What would you like about that difference? What would you hate about that difference?

_____
_____
_____
_____
_____
_____
_____
_____
_____
_____
_____
_____
_____
_____
_____
_____
_____
_____
_____
_____
_____
_____
_____
_____
_____
_____
_____
_____
_____
_____

7. Wonder what makes wish number two so important to you. When was it born? How did it grow to be so connected to who you are? How can you honor yourself and your wish today?

_____

_____

_____

_____

_____

_____

_____

_____

_____

_____

_____

_____

_____

_____

_____

_____

_____

_____

_____

_____

_____

_____

_____

_____

_____

_____

_____

_____

8. *Honor*—does that sound like a foreign term to you? What is honor? What does it mean to honor yourself?

_____

_____

_____

_____

_____

_____

_____

_____

_____

_____

_____

_____

_____

_____

_____

_____

_____

_____

_____

_____

_____

_____

_____

_____

_____

_____

_____

_____

_____

_____

9. Does it make you feel uncomfortable to honor yourself? Why?

_____

_____

_____

_____

_____

_____

_____

_____

_____

_____

_____

_____

_____

_____

_____

_____

_____

_____

_____

_____

_____

_____

_____

_____

_____

_____

_____

_____

10. Who gave you messages about honor in your childhood? How do those messages steal your joy with your successes now?

_____

_____

_____

_____

_____

_____

_____

_____

_____

_____

_____

_____

_____

_____

_____

_____

_____

_____

_____

_____

_____

_____

_____

_____

_____

_____

_____

_____

11. Which feeling gets in the way of wish number two? Write about that feeling.

_____

_____

_____

_____

_____

_____

_____

_____

_____

_____

_____

_____

_____

_____

_____

_____

_____

_____

_____

_____

_____

_____

_____

_____

_____

_____

_____

_____

_____

12. When was the first time you had that feeling? What do you remember about that event?

_____

_____

_____

_____

_____

_____

_____

_____

_____

_____

_____

_____

_____

_____

_____

_____

_____

_____

_____

_____

_____

_____

_____

_____

_____

_____

_____

13. What other feelings come up as you remember the event?

_____

_____

_____

_____

_____

_____

_____

_____

_____

_____

_____

_____

_____

_____

_____

_____

_____

_____

_____

_____

_____

_____

_____

_____

_____

_____

_____

_____

Feelings to Explore

Accepted	Good	Resentful
Afraid	Guilty	Sad
Annoyed	Happy	Safe
Anxious	Helpless	Sensual
Angry	Hopeful	Sentimental
Ashamed	Hostile	Sexual
Bewildered	Humiliated	Shaky
Bitter	Hurt	Shy
Bored	Inadequate	Strong
Brave	Intense	Subdued
Confident	Intimidated	Tender
Confused	Irritable	Tense
Defeated	Jazzed	Terrified
Defensive	Jealous	Tired
Depressed	Lonely	Trapped
Detached	Loving	Ugly
Disappointed	Mean	Uneasy
Disgusted	Miserable	Unwelcome
Disturbed	Needed	Uptight
Edgy	Neglected	Vulnerable
Embarrassed	Passionate	Warm
Enthusiastic	Pessimistic	Weak
Envious	Playful	Wonderful
Ecstatic	Pleased	Worried
Fearful	Protective	
Foolish	Puzzled	
Frustrated	Rejected	
Furious	Relieved	

14. Choose three feelings that you are aware of from the above list and explore them. Start by defining them. What does it mean to feel "X"?

_____
_____
_____
_____
_____
_____
_____
_____
_____
_____
_____
_____
_____
_____
_____
_____
_____
_____
_____
_____
_____
_____
_____
_____
_____
_____

15. How do you act when you are feeling "X"? Do you like that behavior? What does "X" feeling need from you? How are you going to meet "X's" needs?

_____

_____

_____

_____

_____

_____

_____

_____

_____

_____

_____

_____

_____

_____

_____

_____

_____

_____

_____

_____

_____

_____

_____

_____

_____

_____

_____

_____

_____

16. Allow yourself to drift into a positive feeling, such as enthusiasm. When was the last time you were enthusiastic? What makes you enthusiastic? How can you invite enthusiasm to be more a part of your daily life?

_____
_____
_____
_____
_____
_____
_____
_____
_____
_____
_____
_____
_____
_____
_____
_____
_____
_____
_____
_____
_____
_____
_____
_____
_____
_____
_____
_____
_____

17. What made your family get enthusiastic? Did you enjoy that? If so, why? If not, why not?

_____

_____

_____

_____

_____

_____

_____

_____

_____

_____

_____

_____

_____

_____

_____

_____

_____

_____

_____

_____

_____

_____

_____

_____

_____

_____

_____

18. If you could allow enthusiasm more access to your daily life, how do you think that will help with obtaining wish number two?

_____

_____

_____

_____

_____

_____

_____

_____

_____

_____

_____

_____

_____

_____

_____

_____

_____

_____

_____

_____

_____

_____

_____

_____

_____

_____

_____

19. What was wish number three? Write it out. How does the lack of personal honor keep you from obtaining wish number three?

_____

_____

_____

_____

_____

_____

_____

_____

_____

_____

_____

_____

_____

_____

_____

_____

_____

_____

_____

_____

_____

_____

_____

_____

_____

_____

_____

_____

_____

_____

20. How would your life be different if wish number three were fulfilled?

_____
_____
_____
_____
_____
_____
_____
_____
_____
_____
_____
_____
_____
_____
_____
_____
_____
_____
_____
_____
_____
_____
_____
_____
_____
_____

21. Is that fact or fantasy? How do you know the difference?

22.Are you still waiting for someone else or some external power to make your wishes come true? If so, who is powerful enough to bring those wishes into your life?

_____

_____

_____

_____

_____

_____

_____

_____

_____

_____

_____

_____

_____

_____

_____

_____

_____

_____

_____

_____

_____

_____

_____

_____

_____

_____

_____

_____

23. Why do you give that person or deity so much power? Does that make you a victim? A person, identifies as a victim, when they feel helpless and powerless. From that perspective, it becomes everyone else's fault and someone else's responsibility to fix it. This type of thinking will likely keep you stuck.

_____

_____

_____

_____

_____

_____

_____

_____

_____

_____

_____

_____

_____

_____

_____

_____

_____

_____

_____

_____

_____

_____

_____

_____

_____

_____

24. Examine the benefits of remaining a victim. What are they for you?

_____

_____

_____

_____

_____

_____

_____

_____

_____

_____

_____

_____

_____

_____

_____

_____

_____

_____

_____

_____

_____

_____

_____

_____

_____

_____

_____

_____

25. As an adult, are you willing to stay in that dependent place? When you were a child growing up in your family, you were truly dependent on them. Often we forget to grow emotionally into our chronological age. We stay at the age at which we were wounded. That is fairly natural; however, you have cleared some emotional space by writing about your anger, helplessness, hope, trust, body, and spirituality. Now you have room to own your own life and have power to make different choices. You can stop waiting on someone else to fulfill your wish list and take more assertive and positive action toward making those wishes become a reality. It is at this point you become clear on how important your desires and wishes are when you are ready to reach out and obtain those wishes. Write about how this challenge makes you feel.

26. Write about your anxiety and fears generated by the call to action. Write about your hope and courage that helped you survive past issues and move forward into your new self.

_____

_____

_____

_____

_____

_____

_____

_____

_____

_____

_____

_____

_____

_____

_____

_____

_____

_____

_____

_____

_____

_____

_____

_____

_____

_____

_____

_____

_____

27. Write a letter to wish number three. Tell it how you are going to achieve it and bring it into fullness. Apologize to it for waiting on someone or something else to birth it. Communicate the joy, hope, and love that you are anticipating as wish number three is born.

_____

_____

_____

_____

_____

_____

_____

_____

_____

_____

_____

_____

_____

_____

_____

_____

_____

_____

_____

_____

_____

_____

_____

_____

_____

_____

_____

28. Write a letter to wish number two. Express your gratitude to it for sticking around and waiting for you to attend to it. Explain to wish number two why it is so important to you.

_____

_____

_____

_____

_____

_____

_____

_____

_____

_____

_____

_____

_____

_____

_____

_____

_____

_____

_____

_____

_____

_____

_____

_____

_____

_____

29. Affirm your need to see it come into being. Tell wish number two how you are going to help bring it into reality.

_____
_____
_____
_____
_____
_____
_____
_____
_____
_____
_____
_____
_____
_____
_____
_____
_____
_____
_____
_____
_____
_____
_____
_____
_____
_____
_____

30. We have now come full circle. Wish number one is waiting for a letter from you. Perhaps by now, wish number one has been fulfilled. Perhaps not. As you reflect on wish number one, take time to reflect over the pages you have written in this journal. Which was your most healing exercise? Why?

31. Which was your most difficult exercise and why?

_____

_____

_____

_____

_____

_____

_____

_____

_____

_____

_____

_____

_____

_____

_____

_____

_____

_____

_____

_____

_____

_____

_____

_____

_____

_____

_____

_____

_____

_____

_____

_____

32. As you reflect on your written pages, what did you learn about the family in which you grew up?

_____

_____

_____

_____

_____

_____

_____

_____

_____

_____

_____

_____

_____

_____

_____

_____

_____

_____

_____

_____

_____

_____

_____

_____

_____

_____

_____

_____

33. What did you learn about your mother that you had not thought of before?

_____
_____
_____
_____
_____
_____
_____
_____
_____
_____
_____
_____
_____
_____
_____
_____
_____
_____
_____
_____
_____
_____
_____
_____
_____
_____
_____
_____
_____

34. If you were going to write your mother a closing letter about what it was like growing up as her child, what would you tell her?

_____
_____
_____
_____
_____
_____
_____
_____
_____
_____
_____
_____
_____
_____
_____
_____
_____
_____
_____
_____
_____
_____
_____
_____
_____
_____
_____
_____

35. Is there anything else you need or want to say to her that will feel like bringing closure to old wounds and hurtful feelings?

_____

_____

_____

_____

_____

_____

_____

_____

_____

_____

_____

_____

_____

_____

_____

_____

_____

_____

_____

_____

_____

_____

_____

_____

_____

_____

36. What feelings are hanging around about your father? What did you come to understand about him that you had not allowed yourself to feel before?

_____

_____

_____

_____

_____

_____

_____

_____

_____

_____

_____

_____

_____

_____

_____

_____

_____

_____

_____

_____

_____

_____

_____

_____

_____

_____

37. What do you wish would have been different between the two of you?

_____

_____

_____

_____

_____

_____

_____

_____

_____

_____

_____

_____

_____

_____

_____

_____

_____

_____

_____

_____

_____

_____

_____

_____

_____

_____

_____

_____

_____

38. If you were going to write a letter to your father, what would be the most important thing to share with him? Why? Dear Dad …

_____

_____

_____

_____

_____

_____

_____

_____

_____

_____

_____

_____

_____

_____

_____

_____

_____

_____

_____

_____

_____

_____

_____

_____

_____

_____

_____

39. What did your parents teach you about committed relationships, such as marriage? Spoken or unspoken, what did they demonstrate about love, closeness, dependency, etc.?

_____

_____

_____

_____

_____

_____

_____

_____

_____

_____

_____

_____

_____

_____

_____

_____

_____

_____

_____

_____

_____

_____

_____

_____

_____

40. What do you need to give back to them about that teaching?

_____
_____
_____
_____
_____
_____
_____
_____
_____
_____
_____
_____
_____
_____
_____
_____
_____
_____
_____
_____
_____
_____
_____
_____
_____
_____
_____
_____

41. What can you take forward into this next year from their teaching about relationships?

_____
_____
_____
_____
_____
_____
_____
_____
_____
_____
_____
_____
_____
_____
_____
_____
_____
_____
_____
_____
_____
_____
_____
_____
_____
_____
_____
_____
_____
_____

42. What else do you need to reflect on and write about before moving onto that letter to wish number one? Perhaps you need to list the feelings that are lingering, the ideas and questions you've yet to address about your life in order to take those questions into your next journal.

_____
_____
_____
_____
_____
_____
_____
_____
_____
_____
_____
_____
_____
_____
_____
_____
_____
_____
_____
_____
_____
_____
_____
_____
_____
_____
_____
_____

43. Write some questions you wish I had asked but did not ask.

_____

_____

_____

_____

_____

_____

_____

_____

_____

_____

_____

_____

_____

_____

_____

_____

_____

_____

_____

_____

_____

_____

_____

_____

_____

_____

_____

_____

44. Write your responses to the questions that you created.

_____
_____
_____
_____
_____
_____
_____
_____
_____
_____
_____
_____
_____
_____
_____
_____
_____
_____
_____
_____
_____
_____
_____
_____
_____
_____
_____
_____
_____

45. Write a letter to wish number one as it was listed in the beginning of your journal. How have you changed? How has that wish changed since you started this process?

_____
_____
_____
_____
_____
_____
_____
_____
_____
_____
_____
_____
_____
_____
_____
_____
_____
_____
_____
_____
_____
_____
_____
_____
_____
_____
_____
_____
_____

46. Write a closing letter to yourself and explore how it is different from the very first letter you wrote.

Date: _____

Dear Self,

_____
_____
_____
_____
_____
_____
_____
_____
_____
_____
_____
_____
_____
_____
_____
_____
_____
_____
_____
_____
_____
_____
_____
_____
_____
_____
_____
_____

This is Not the End, but the Beginning of Your Next Step!

You have come to the end of this journal. I hope you found it thought-provoking and helpful throughout your process, regardless of how long it has taken or how you decided to use it. I sincerely hope it has been a useful tool in getting to know yourself and your history within the context of your story and your three wishes.

Now that you have invested time and energy in this process, where will you go from here? What is next for you? What is stirring inside? Is it time for you to see a professional to help you sort and sift through what came up for you, if you have not already done so? Is it time to start a new journal to write about what is next for you?

There are many books and tools out there that can be helpful as you move forward in your life. In addition to this journal, I have a smaller workbook of lessons from *The Miller's Daughter, Miller's Daughter* Kindle edition, and my premier work, *In a Moment's Notice: A Psychologist's Journey with Breast Cancer.* Not a book on how to survive cancer, *In a Moment's Notice* is my personal story and journey with cancer that will introduce you to new concepts, such as labyrinths as a healing meditation and guided imagery tools. Order your copies today at Amazon.com.

Sincerely,
Dr. Robin B. Dilley

Printed in the United States
By Bookmasters